Santa Claus
Is for
Real

CHARLES EDWARD HALL

THE RADIO CITY CHRISTMAS SPECTACULAR SANTA

WITH *NEW YORK TIMES* BESTSELLING AUTHOR

BRET WITTER

G

GALLERY BOOKS

NEW YORK   LONDON   TORONTO   SYDNEY   NEW DELHI

Santa Claus

Is for

Real

A True Christmas Fable
About the Magic of Believing

G

Gallery Books
An Imprint of Simon & Schuster, Inc.
1230 Avenue of the Americas
New York, NY 10020

This Gallery Books trade paperback edition December 2022

GALLERY BOOKS and colophon are registered trademarks of
Simon & Schuster, Inc.

For information about special discounts for bulk purchases,
please contact Simon & Schuster Special Sales at 1-866-506-1949
or business@simonandschuster.com.

The Simon & Schuster Speakers Bureau can bring authors to your
live event. For more information or to book an event, contact
the Simon & Schuster Speakers Bureau at 1-866-248-3049
or visit our website at www.simonspeakers.com.

Manufactured in the United States of America

10   9   8   7   6   5   4   3   2   1

Library of Congress Cataloging-in-Publication Data is available.

ISBN 978-1-4767-4373-8
ISBN 978-1-6680-2491-1 (pbk)
ISBN 978-1-4767-4375-2 (ebook)

*To Mom and Dad
who always made Christmas special*

Santa Claus
Is for
Real

An Invitation

O nce upon a time, for that is how all Christmas stories should begin, there was a man who believed with all his heart in Santa Claus. He believed in the Santa who brought presents to all little boys and girls, the good ones and even the just-good-once-in-a-while ones. He believed in the Santa who shimmied down the chimney on Christmas Eve, and who somehow managed when the chimney was narrower than a Yule ham, or when there was no chimney at all. He believed in the Santa who brought gifts even when Mom and Dad couldn't afford the car payment and the electricity was shut off. He believed in the Santa who wanted every little boy and girl to feel special at least once a year. A Santa who knew that it wasn't the gifts that mattered, but the delight and anticipation and wonder in a young child's heart.

He believed in another Santa as well, not the jolly old elf guiding his reindeer from the North Pole, but a Santa who's a bit harder to pin down. This Santa was the Spirit of Christmas, and he wasn't just one person. He was the young woman who dropped not just a quarter but a five-dollar bill into the homeless man's cup. The grandfather who picked up an extra bag of food at the grocery store so other families could have a nice holiday meal. The mother who bought a coat and a video game for a child she didn't know, so another mother could feel like a hero on Christmas morning. The grown man who called the brother he hadn't seen in years with words of peace and love. This was the Santa we could all become: the special people who let children sit on their laps and tell them what they want for Christmas, because, let's face it, the actual Big Man is a little too busy to make it to each and every mall.

This man, the one I'm writing about, is one of those stand-in Santas himself. For twenty-seven Christmases, he has walked onto the stage at Radio City Music Hall in New York City and shared a message of hope and love with New Yorkers and visitors alike. He has performed in a show like no other, not just a Christmas play but a Spectacular, a celebration of the magic of the season. Along with his fellow actors, the Rockettes, the singers, and hundreds of others behind the scenes, he tries to bring joy and wonder to a busy world. He dances and sings and, hopefully, he awakens a little bit of Santa Claus in the hearts of his audience.

But it wasn't always that way. Sometimes we forget the magic around us, the magic that's here not just at Christmas but all of the year, and we don't feel Santa in our hearts. We don't feel kindness and generosity and love. We forget, in other words, why we're here.

I know it happens. I know it's *easy* for it to happen. Because it happened to me. My name is Charles Edward Hall, and I am that Radio City Music Hall Santa, and this is the story of how I became Santa Claus.

Because when I started at Radio City, I wasn't Santa at all.

I was Scrooge.

CHAPTER

1

When we are children, it's easy to believe in Santa, both the man from the North Pole and the one inside each of us. We realize that maybe once or twice we pushed our brother and told Dad he started it, that we broke a friend's toy and tried to hide the evidence, and that it's possible we took an extra cookie when Mom wasn't looking. We know we aren't perfect, but that basically we're good. And if we aren't entirely sure even of that, we know that at least one other person believes in us. We see the proof on Christmas morning, and if the Big Man has put us on the good list once again, we trust that he knows best.

So it isn't so surprising, I suppose, that I met Santa for the first time when I was a child. It was the year of the big snow. A North Pole–worthy snow. I was six years old, and I was so excited I ran out into the storm without a heavy coat or hat to cover my head. It was late afternoon on Christmas Eve, and the snow was ten feet high. Or at least that's how it seemed to this small-town Kentucky boy.

I didn't stop to admire it. I swiped a handful of snow off the front porch railing, packing it into a ball as I ran. I paused halfway across the front yard, my breath steaming. The snow was blowing so hard I could barely make out the house across the street. I whipped the snowball at our mailbox, but halfway there it disappeared into the storm.

My nose was cold. My fingers ached, because I wasn't wearing gloves. I looked back at my house, where the Christmas lights twinkled along the roofline and around the front door. Big, colorful lights with big bulbs. I remember the Christmas tree in the front window and, on the floor above, my brother watching from our shared bedroom window.

I thought about turning back, but instead I sprinted down the street, through the stand of trees I used to think was a forest and up the big hill near the bend in the road. At the top, I fell onto my knees, then onto my back. I stretched out my arms and stared up at the sky. It was blank and white. I moved my arms back and forth in the snow, slowly at first, then faster, forming the wings of a snow angel.

"Believe," I heard someone say.

"Believe in what?" I yelled, my breath puffing out like smoke.

"Believe in goodness," a man said, staring down at me. "Believe in joy. Believe in me, if you want. But believe."

I was scared out of my wits, and I'm not proud to say that I took the Lord's name in vain.

"No," he said. "I never claimed to be him. I'm just a friend."

He looked at me lying there in the snow, in my little snow angel, and laughed. It was a laugh that sounded like it came from somewhere deep inside of him, and it really did make his belly shake like a bowlful of jelly. When I heard that laugh, I could feel the warmth spreading to the tips of my fingers.

Then I saw another face behind him. A small face, like a child's, but with a long, dark brown beard. "Let's go," the elf said. "It's Christmas Eve."

And the next thing I knew, he was gone.

But I saw him again a few hours later. I was sitting in the living room, a cup of hot chocolate warming my tingling fingers, when I heard the crunch of tires on the driveway. Then footsteps on the walk.

"Think fast," my teenage cousin said, flinging a present at me as he burst through the front door.

"Thanks," I said, catching the gift and ripping off the paper. I showed the football to Mom, who was standing in the kitchen doorway, and Dad, who was behind her with a drink in his hand. Mom smiled. "How nice," she said.

Dad turned away, so I did, too. And that's when I saw it. A movement in the window.

A red hat.

A beard.

I heard the sound of a bell.

Then, nothing.

I stared. Hoping, hoping . . . and there he was again. For a second, we looked at each other. Then he nodded, put his finger to his nose. I heard the bell again, and he disappeared.

I was still staring into the darkness when my Uncle

Walt burst into the room, shaking snow off his coat. "Merry Christmas, everyone," he shouted, pulling off his gloves.

He hugged Mom and Dad, laughed happily, then swept me up into his arms, spun me around, and put me back down. He was a big man, and his hands were cold.

"I saw him," I said.

"Who did you see, Charlie?"

"Santa. I saw him in the window. It was him. It was really him."

"Of course it was. Who else would it be?"

That night I lay in bed, wide awake, talking with my big brother. I didn't tell him about the hill—that was my secret—but I told him about what I saw in the window: the hat, the beard, the sound of the bell when he appeared and disappeared. Was the bell on his hat, my brother wondered? Or was it the sound of reindeer?

How had Santa gotten here, anyway? Surely he would have brought Rudolph in such a snowstorm.

Yes, the bell must have been Rudolph . . . but where was the sleigh? And why had he come so early in the

evening? And where was he now? I hesitated. Maybe ...
West Virginia?

My brother lay quietly for a while, thinking. "I don't
believe it," he said finally.

"You don't believe in Santa?" I said.

"Of course I believe in Santa," he said. "I just don't
believe he'd come to see a kid like you."

I realized something then: my big brother didn't
know everything. In fact, I wasn't sure he knew anything at all.

So I stayed quiet, watching the snow. I remember
how big and wonderful the world felt then. How magical. How warm.

When I finally heard my brother snoring, I whispered, "I believe."

Santa Claus had come to Frankfort, Kentucky. He
had looked in my window.

He was real.

CHAPTER

2

H ave you ever struggled to keep your eyes open on Christmas Eve, hoping that this will be the year you catch a glimpse of Santa? Ever lay out a few extra cookies, wishing that maybe he'll stick around, and you'll catch him in the act? Most kids do.

I even know some children who set little traps. They sprinkle baby powder by the chimney so they'll see his footsteps, or make an ornament that "accidentally" slips off the tree so he'll make noise when he steps on it, or even bribe their older brothers to wake them up after midnight. While I don't suggest trying to catch Santa with a trip wire or a net—it would be a shame if he spent Christmas Eve in the emergency room rather than delivering gifts—I know lots of children are tempted. They have seen the evidence—half-eaten cookies, scuff marks on the hearth, not to mention the piles of presents—but Santa . . . he still remains a mystery.

So why, with all those kids laying out cookies and milk, did Santa Claus come to see me? That's what all the children ask whenever I tell my story. Why you, Mr. Hall? Why did Santa visit you?

After all, I was just a regular Kentucky kid, not so different from any other boy. My family wasn't rich, and it wasn't poor. The town I lived in wasn't big, but it wasn't small either. I wasn't even that well behaved, although I certainly wasn't bad. In other words, there was nothing special about me.

Was it because of who I would become? Did Santa know that one day that little kid on the hill would become an actor, and that his most famous role would be Santa Claus? Did he know the future? Is that why he came?

When I met Santa later—we'll get to that part, don't worry—I asked him that question.

"No, I didn't know you'd play me," he said, shaking his head. "My magic is Christmas magic. It can get me around the world in one night, and it can keep straight who's been naughty and who's been nice, but it can't tell me the future. Frankly, Charlie, I never thought we'd meet again."

It was an accident, that's all; it could have happened to anyone. Santa was just passing by. He saw me in the snow and he knew me, because of course Santa knows every child. And he knew I needed his help. That's part of who Santa is, and now I'm talking about both the Big Man and the Santa inside of us. When Santa sees someone in need, he helps.

You see, I really did need Santa's help. Like a lot of kids, not every day was Christmas for me, and I needed to hold on to the spirit. My father was a drinker. He never spent time with my brother or me, and eventually my big brother dealt with his hurt by beating up on me. He pushed me down the stairs and laughed. He punched me until I bruised, and then punched me right on the bruises themselves. He played cruel tricks that left me in tears, and no one ever said a word. But whenever I felt hurt and alone, I would remember that the world was bigger than my little house, and that someone out there cared.

I knew Santa was there, in other words. I knew it,

even if I only saw glimpses of him once in a while. Like in the fifth grade, when a new teacher, Phil Bryan, heard me give an oral book report and said, "You've got a good voice, Charlie. You should try out for the Thanksgiving play."

Really? I thought. You think I'm good at something? I don't think I'd ever had an adult believe in me before.

So I tried out.

I didn't get the lead part. Doug Martin was chosen to play the talking turkey, of course, because he was smarter and more popular. In fact, he was the smartest and most popular boy at Thorn Hill Elementary. He wore nice pants instead of jeans; he brought his lunch from home, while the rest of us ate school food; and he chewed that lunch in such a way that every kid knew exactly how good it tasted. Everybody liked Doug Martin, and everybody wanted to be like Doug Martin, because Doug Martin could do anything.

I played the Indian Chief. And though it wasn't the biggest role, I practiced my lines every day. Even before the show, I knew I was better at this than even Doug Martin, because he was terrible at acting. But standing onstage in front of all those parents, wearing my big feathered headdress, I almost lost my nerve.

Until I looked into the audience and saw Santa's face. It was just a poster for an upcoming Christmas play, but when I saw Santa smiling, I knew his spirit was there. And I believed.

I believed in myself.

A few weeks later, I was in the kitchen at our little house when a distant relative named Martha Conway walked in and saw me standing there all alone.

"So what do you want be when you grow up, Charlie?" she asked, trying to make conversation.

I didn't even think about it. "I'm going to be an actor in New York City," I told her. Mind you, I was a country boy. I didn't even know where New York City was, much less know anything about it. I had just heard somewhere that that's where actors lived. So I said it.

And Martha Conway laughed, right in my ten-year-old face. She didn't mean to hurt my feelings, it was just so unexpected she couldn't help herself. "Now where," she asked, "would a boy from Frankfort, Kentucky, get an idea like that?"

CHAPTER
3

I didn't say anything to Martha Conway that day. I just thought, *I don't care what you think. I believe.*

Because I did believe. I said that I was nothing special, but that's not really true. Santa taught me that I was special—because we're all special. Some people can run fast. Some write or draw. Some use their minds for great thoughts and new discoveries. Some spread love to those around them. Each of us has a gift, even if it's not always easy for other people to see. That's part of Santa's magic—he knows us. He sees that special gift inside and keeps us on the good list even if every now and then we throw temper tantrums and take a marker to the living room walls.

Santa doesn't appear to everyone, but that doesn't mean he isn't there. His spirit is around us all. When Phil Bryan told a boy who didn't think much of himself that he had a voice people wanted to hear, that was Santa speaking. When I was nervous, and I spotted that poster across the room, that was Santa, too. And of course the man I spoke to on that hill was Santa Claus, and if he believed in me, who was I to argue?

That belief in myself took me all the way from Thorn Hill Elementary to Murray State University in western Kentucky, and then Maryland and upstate New York, and finally, just like I had told Martha Conway when I was ten years old, to New York City.

The city back then was a pretty scary place, I have to admit. Run-down buildings. Dog waste on the sidewalks. Graffiti so thick on the subway cars you couldn't see out the windows. Crime was high, the city was broke, and the federal government had told it, in the memorable words of a local newspaper, to "drop dead."

Go to Times Square today, the heart of the theater district, and you'll find magic: big beautiful theaters, fantastic lights, thousands of happy people flocking to see *Annie* and *The Lion King* and even *Spider-Man*. But Times Square wasn't always that way. When I arrived, it was full of con men, trinket stores, and movie halls so dingy you would never go inside. Most of the famous theaters, including Radio City Music Hall, were boarded up. Instead of music coming from the orchestra pits, homeless people were building fires out of torn-up seats.

Still, for three years I went to Times Square every day. The city may have been down and dirty, but this was still New York City. There were still a few serious plays, and the only place to try out for them was Actors' Equity Hall. Four or five days a week, at 5 a.m., I'd walk two miles uptown to stand in line. If you weren't in line by 6 a.m., the wait for a three-minute interview with a casting director could take all day. If you passed the interview, you came back the next week for an audition. I went to two hundred interviews the first year and received three callbacks. Most days, I trudged home empty-handed, except for a hunk of cheese and a loaf of day-old bread I bought for half price at the bus station.

For a while, I'd look at the skyscrapers and think New York was the most beautiful place on earth. I'd like to say I kept Santa's magic in my heart, that through all those hard times, I remembered the wonder. But I didn't.

Over the years, I lost my way. I stopped looking at the tall buildings and saw only the road in front of me.

I still believed, but now it was only in hard work. And making it. That's what they call it when you can go home and say, "See, I did what you said I never could." And I did make it. First, I landed a role in Walt Disney's *Snow White*. Then a touring musical, then a real Broadway show. For five years, I had health insurance and money in my pocket.

These are all good things, right? Of course!

But in the midst of all those good things, I lost something important: Santa Claus.

I wish that weren't true. I wish that after I met Santa he stayed in my heart forever. But like a lot of adults, I got so busy with other things, I forgot about Christmas magic. I didn't become a bad person. I didn't push old ladies on the sidewalk or rob banks. I just stopped caring about Christmas morning and flying reindeer and waking up to snow on your windowsill.

I started believing in success so much that all I cared about was success. I forgot the most important things in life: wonder and joy.

CHAPTER

4

I didn't want to be in the *Radio City Christmas Spectacular*. That's the honest truth.

I wanted to be in a serious Broadway play. I wanted to be a highly respected actor. But in those days, there weren't so many serious plays on Broadway. The only thing a young actor like me could really count on was musicals. And I hated musicals.

All that singing and dancing. All that smiling and joy. All that . . . good cheer. Bah, humbug.

But my last show had ended, and I'd been out of work for two years. I didn't have any more money, and I didn't have any health insurance. I was eating Cheerios and living in a two-room apartment with nothing but a sleeping bag, a crate for my clothes, and my guitar. So when I heard Bob Yanni, an old friend who had produced *Snow White,* was looking to hire someone for the

Radio City Christmas Spectacular, I swallowed my pride.

Besides, this wasn't just any role I was trying out for. This was the star of the show, the Big Man, the greatest character in the history of Christmas.

That's right . . . Ebenezer Scrooge.

Now you probably think of Scrooge as a mean man who hated Christmas. And he was. But he wasn't evil. In fact, I don't think he ever wanted to be bad. He just had a hard childhood and a broken heart, and he lost his way. He forgot that being nice is better than being rich. That's why he becomes good in the end, after the visit from the third ghost, because he had been good all along. He just didn't know it. He had lost his faith.

So that's how I auditioned for Scrooge: as a disappointed man who had forgotten how to believe. I muttered, "Humbug on Christmas." I snarled, "Leave me be." And at the end, I fell on my knees and cried, "Please, please spirit, give me another chance."

And do you know what Bob Yanni said?

He said, "That's fine, Charlie. Thank you." I thought he was going to pass.

Then he stopped. "You know, the actor playing Scrooge has two parts this year. We've written a few scenes for Santa Claus, and I want the same actor to play them both."

"Santa Claus?"

"You know: fat guy, jolly old elf."

I hadn't thought of Santa since moving to New York City, but as soon as Mr. Yanni said his name, I remembered that Christmas Eve when I was six years old. I remembered the feeling of wonder and joy.

"I love Santa," I said. "If you give me the script, I can audition right now."

Mr. Yanni shook his head. "Why don't you make something up?" he said. "I'd love to see what you think of him."

What do I think of him? What do I think about Santa? To my surprise, I didn't know. I wasn't sure what to say . . . until I saw him standing in the corner of the room. I had forgotten the magic of Christmas, but Santa had not forgotten me. I swear, that day, Santa put his words right into my mouth, because I don't remember thinking of them, I just remember starting to speak:

Long ago, before there were trees, there was ice, and snow, and the spirit of Christmas. And there was Santa Claus.

At first, I was a feeling. Then an idea. And finally, five hundred years ago, I became a man. I haven't always had this beard. And I haven't always had this belly. But I have always had this laugh: ho-ho-ho. And I have always had this smile.

I have been doing this a long time. I have given millions of gifts. You remember that wooden horse, don't you, Bobby? And that book about dinosaurs? And those video games you just had to have the year you turned ten?

But even after all these years, I've only really given one gift. And that gift is joy.

So come with me, friends. Let's dance and sing. Let's celebrate. It's not hard. All you do is put your lips together and hum. Then it gets in your toes, and they start tapping. And your fingers start snapping. And then you feel it, right here. In your heart. The magic of Christmas.

I felt a hand on my shoulder. Santa Claus? No, he had disappeared. It was Bob Yanni, who had gotten up out of his chair. "Can you come back tomorrow?" he said. "I want you to meet Mrs. Claus."

"Does that mean I got the job?"

"Yes, Charles, you got the job."

I was so excited, I floated all the way home to my apartment building. I ran up the five flights of stairs. I burst through the door and shouted to no one in particular, because there was nobody there but me: "I got the part! I got the part! I'm Ebenezer Scrooge!"

CHAPTER

5

I woke up in the middle of the night. An enormous man was standing at the foot of my bed. Now, that would be enough to send any normal person screaming for the police, but, somehow I felt safe, for he was the kind of man who makes you laugh in spite of yourself when you see him, even in the middle of the night in New York City. He had a thick beard and wore an enormous coat. He looked kind of like my Uncle Walter.

I pinched myself to see if I was dreaming. It hurt, and the big man didn't disappear. So I asked him who he was.

He didn't answer.

"What is your name?"

No reply.

"What do you want?"

He laughed. "I want to help you, Charlie."

"Why?"

"Because I believe in you."

"Is that why you are here?"

"I've always been here, Charlie. Don't you remember?"

I thought of the audition, and how the words popped out of my mouth before I realized I was saying them. "Are you here to help me achieve fame and fortune?"

He sighed and shook his head.

I waited, expecting more. I stared at him until my eyes began to droop, hoping he would tell me something important, but . . . nothing. Nothing at all.

I guess there was nothing more to say.

CHAPTER
6

Wwhat kind of fool turns down Santa Claus? That's crazy, right? But that's the kind of fool I was. I was twenty-nine years old. I was arrogant. And I was determined to make something of myself. I didn't come to New York City to play Santa Claus. I came to be famous and successful and to show those people in Frankfort, Kentucky, that they couldn't kick Charlie Hall down anymore.

Santa was too easy for a professional like me. All he did was laugh. He was jolly. He helped people. Being good all the time was easy, I thought. Smile. Dance. Ho-ho-ho. Nobody was going to win a Tony Award for that.

Ebenezer Scrooge, now he was a character. Angry. Scared. Brave. Remorseful. Excited. And, most important, redeemed. Scrooge was an award winner, because

Scrooge changed. With Ebenezer Scrooge, the most important part wasn't the bah, humbugs. The most important part was when he fell on his knees and cried for a second chance.

Besides, Santa Claus was such a simple version of Christmas: goodness, happiness, giving, blah blah blah.

Scrooge was something else: proof that the spirit of Christmas can redeem a disappointing world. It can make you the person you always wanted to be.

Or it can change someone you love.

Haven't you always wanted that?

I have. Every year as a kid, I went to bed on Christmas Eve hoping the world would be better in the morning. That my mother would be happier. That my father would stop drinking. That my big brother would stop punching me.

Every year, I wanted Ebenezer Scrooge's Christmas miracle.

But it never happened. My father lost his job. My brother mocked me. Many nights, I lay awake and listened to my mother cry herself to sleep.

So every year, I became a little more like "Humbug Scrooge." I tied pots and pans to my father while he slept, then woke him up and laughed as he stumbled around, trying to catch me. I talked back to my teachers. One year, a boy threw a rock at me while I was riding my bike. Instead of riding away, as I always had before, I turned around and started pedaling toward him. He saw me coming and reached for a metal pipe that was lying alongside the road. He came up swinging, but before he could turn I hit him dead center without slowing down.

It was like the universe burst open, and I could hear it screaming. I turned back to look. The kid was lying motionless on the ground, and behind him a woman was running across a grassy yard, and I knew it was his mother screaming, not the universe, because the sound stopped when she fainted. She thought I had killed her son, and for a moment I thought I had, too.

But I wasn't that scared little kid anymore. Now I was the lead actor in a Broadway show, and there was no way I was going to let anyone throw rocks at me.

This is it, Charlie Hall, I told myself. The part you were meant to play.

And yet every night I dreamed of Santa and his sad smile when I asked if he'd bring me fame and fortune.

He had a message for me, I knew that. But I was living the dream, I thought I was happy, and I didn't want to hear about anything else.

So every night I just rolled over and went back to sleep.

CHAPTER 7

We started rehearsals with one of my Santa scenes: the opening number for the show. Santa was planning his trip with Mrs. Claus at the North Pole, while his elves prepared the sleigh. It wasn't until halfway through that the audience realized he wasn't going on his Christmas Eve journey, he was going to Radio City Music Hall.

And that's when the singing and dancing started. Ugh. I hated that about musical theater: one minute you're doing a serious acting scene, and the next you've broken into a song that describes exactly what you were doing the minute before.

"I'm going to the store, tra-la-la. I'm going to buy some candy, tra-la-la. I hope they have grape, for goodness sake, because lemon is such a bore."

Exactly like real life, isn't it?

The craziest part of the scene wasn't the singing, though, and it wasn't the eight elves that sang along with me. It was Mat Mat the reindeer.

"Where did you get this deer?" I yelled to no one in particular after the first two frustrating hours. "He smells like a barn."

We couldn't see the director because the theater was so big, but we could hear him over the public address system: "He lives in a barn, Charles. He's a trained animal. Now let's try that again."

Hour after hour, Mat Mat missed his cues. He walked when he was supposed to stand. He stood when he was supposed to pull. He should have gone straight across the stage, with the elves running beside him, but he kept chasing the elves instead.

"Thank God I'm not in the sleigh today," I muttered to Randy, the stagehand who was supposed to be controlling him. "You're going to kill me with that animal."

Finally, half an hour before the end of rehearsal, Mat Mat caught poor John Edward, who was playing Hans the Elf, and snatched off his elf hat. When Randy dropped the reins to retrieve it, Mat Mat charged another stagehand, Petey, who was standing off to the side minding his own business, and got his antlers tangled in the curtain ropes.

Then he snorted at Mrs. Claus, stink-eyed the director, and let loose his droppings right on my shoe.

"Clean that up," I snapped at Randy. It had been a long day, but I stood there until Randy had my shoe good and clean.

It was eight o'clock by the time Mat Mat was back in his trailer, so the elves and I went out to dinner.

They were a great group of men and women, with fantastic stories about plays they'd been in, tours they'd done, and all the times people were jerks or underestimated them or treated them badly.

"It wasn't very Santa-like of you," someone said.

I looked down. It was David, by far the smallest of the actors playing my elves. In the sleigh scene, he played Mr. Spruce, who was sort of like Santa's butler. Mr. Spruce's job was to straighten Santa's coat and wipe the cookie crumbs out of his beard.

"What are you talking about, David?" I asked.

"When you made Randy clean reindeer poop off your shoe. Santa's not like that."

"Well, I wasn't playing Santa then, David. I was just being myself."

"I'm just saying. In case you're interested."

"What I'm interested in right now," I said, getting up from my stool, "is meeting Becky Morrow. We have a date tonight."

"Who's Becky?"

"The prettiest woman in the chorus, of course."

"Is that important?" he asked. "That she's prettiest, I mean."

I looked at David. Was he being serious? Of course it was important.

"David," I said, sitting back down. "Let me tell you a story. When Snow White was being cast, I tried out for the prince. I didn't get the role, because they said I wasn't handsome enough. So what role did I get? The wicked witch. That's right. I played the ugly old woman. But do you know what? I not only dated Snow White, I married her."

"How did that turn out?"

"The fairy tale didn't last. We divorced. It broke my heart."

"I'm sorry to hear that," David said.

"That's not the point, David. The point is that now I'm the star, and the star dates the prettiest woman in the show."

"You know," David said as I put on my coat to leave. "That's not like Santa Claus either."

"Thank you, David. I'll keep that in mind. Good night."

CHAPTER
8

CHAPTER

8

A few days later, we started working on Scrooge, which was a relief. I was troubled by what David had said, that I needed to act like Santa Claus, even when I wasn't playing Santa Claus. That felt like a lot of pressure. Santa was always good. And he was always jolly. I wasn't ready for all of that.

But Scrooge? I could be as much of a grump as I wanted, and nobody would say a word. That's sort of the problem. It's quite easy to be angry and make excuses, because life is complicated. Something always goes wrong, and doesn't it make you feel good to get mad about it and blame others?

At least for a little while.

The problem was the props. Scrooge was supposed to be the star of the show, but Santa's part was so elaborate, with the dancing elves and Mat Mat the Crazy

Reindeer, that the director decided Scrooge needed something spectacular, too.

Scrooge needed to fly.

"Are you sure about this?" I asked John Lemac, the lead stagehand, as he strapped me into the flying device. It was just a harness that went around my waist and between my legs. I looked up and saw the wires climbing fifty feet to a pulley, then across to another pulley, then down to a stagehand holding the other end.

"Just don't lose your lunch," John said, as another stagehand pulled down on the wire, jerking me into the air. "It's a little unsettling the first time."

Unsettling? It was the worst carnival ride of all time. I wobbled. I spun. I tried to regain my balance, turned upside down, and then—holy guacamole!—the stagehand jerked me up and over in a full circle, and before I knew what was happening, I was sick on the floor.

After three days, I was so sore from the flying that I could barely walk home, and I was so angry that I was yelling at the cast and crew. That's when Abbey approached me. Abbey played the Ghost of Christmas Present, who was my partner in the flying scene. Scrooge was supposed to grab the bottom of her dress as she flew away. That's what launched him into the air.

"Do you want to work on the flying?" she asked with a concerned smile. "I have a few tips that might make it easier, and I'm happy to stay after. We can practice together."

"I can't tonight. I have a date."

"I'll stay with you," someone said. I looked around. It was Randy, the stagehand.

"Aren't you on Mat Mat duty?" I asked him.

"No, I got fired from the reindeer. I've been pulling your wire for the last three days. Haven't you noticed?"

"Sorry. I guess not."

He huffed, then turned to Abbey. "I'd love to stay and work the wires for you. And maybe afterward we can get a drink or a bite . . ."

"I tell you what," I said, before she could answer. "Why don't we work on it tomorrow? All three of us. Wouldn't that be swell?"

Abbey looked relieved. Randy smiled like he wanted to bite my nose off. So I smiled back at him.

"Yes," he said. "That would be swell."

"Great. So it's a date."

CHAPTER 9

The workshop scene was classic musical theater. It started with Santa alone on the stage, reading a letter from a little girl. She wanted a certain doll for Christmas, but she was worried because she couldn't find one anywhere.

"No problem," Santa said, and the curtain flew open to reveal seven elves in a workshop, banging away on toys. Then the music started, and Rockettes dressed as dolls started appearing from the wings of the stage. Within minutes, there were thirty-six Rockettes, seven elves, and Santa dancing and singing in a big musical number. The music swelled, the Rockettes kicked, and just as the song ended, Santa opened a cupboard to get that perfect doll for that lovely little girl.

And out popped David, my shortest elf.

He threw his arms in the air, jumped to the floor,

and danced his way to the front of the stage. I almost lost my beard I laughed so hard. The guy was a born showman. This, I thought, is what musical theater is all about.

"You were magnificent out there," I told David after the rehearsal. "Where did you learn those moves?"

He shrugged. "I've been doing this a long time."

I saw Linda Lemac, the company manager, approaching across the stage. "They want you on the local news, Charlie," she said. "Show promotion. Early holiday piece. Do you think you can be ready in an hour?"

"Do they want Santa? Or do they want Scrooge?"

She looked at me with exasperation. "Of course they don't want Scrooge. Nobody wants Scrooge. They want Santa."

Well, it wasn't national, and it wasn't the serious dramatic part I craved, but still, it was television . . .

"Maybe I should come along," David said.

Linda looked at me with a worried expression, like she expected me to angrily tell David to take a hike.

"I agree," I said, to her clear surprise. "Santa should bring his elf. Have you seen this guy perform? He's a genius."

Thank goodness I had David along, because I wasn't even close to prepared. It turns out, I didn't know anything about Santa Claus. Oh, I knew he rode in a sleigh, and that he had eight reindeer, and that he lived at the North Pole. But how did he spend this time in November?

"Mostly relaxing," David told the reporter. "It's us elves that do all the work."

Was he excited for Christmas?

"Of course," I said.

"But not as much as the elves," David said. "We finally get a vacation."

And most important, why did he decide to perform at Radio City Music Hall this year?

"Well, I . . . um . . ."

"For the children," David said. "These are hard days in New York City, but Santa's here to remind them about the joy of Christmas."

"How did you do that, David?" I asked him as we left the studio. "You saved my bacon out there."

"I told you," he said. "I've been doing this a long time."

We kept talking as we walked the fifteen or so blocks

to my apartment. I kept asking him, "How should I play the part?"

Should I fall down in surprise when he hopped out of the cabinet?

No, that was too much.

Should I thank him when he straightened and cleaned my coat?

No, Santa was in too much of a hurry during the Christmas season to notice.

When we finally got to my building, I invited him to my apartment. "Five floors up," I said. "Sorry, no elevator."

David grimaced. "It's late," he said. "Maybe I should go home." He looked around, then sighed sadly. "Do you mind hailing me a cab? Sometimes they don't see me."

I signaled for a cab. "You know, Charles," he said, as he climbed in. "Underneath it all, you're a decent guy. I think you're going to be all right."

"Do you have any more advice for me, David? Anything to make my Santa character better?"

He rolled down the window. "Just be good, for goodness' sake," he said as the cab pulled away.

I turned back to my building, and for a moment I thought I saw Santa standing there, just like in my dream. "You again? What do you want now?" I snapped.

"Spare change?" he replied. It was just an old man in a dirty coat, huddled against the first cold night of the year.

"Oh, I'm sorry," I said, reaching into my pocket and giving him a dollar bill.

"Bless you, sir," he said, and for a moment I thought I saw a twinkle in his eye.

CHAPTER
10

T he next day, when I arrived home from rehearsals, Santa was sitting in my only comfortable chair, waiting for me. Somehow it seemed like the most natural thing in the world, like arriving home and finding your crazy uncle's RV parked in the driveway. Of course it was going to happen that way. How else could the world work?

"Good evening, Charlie," he said.

"Hey, Santa," I said. "I guess I was expecting you."

He was wearing his giant coat, and in the full light of the evening he was bigger than I remembered. I said before he was like my Uncle Walter, but up close he was more like Hagrid from the Harry Potter movies. He was bushy and looked like he could barely fit through the doorway.

"Do you have any milk?" he asked. "And I hope you have some cookies."

"I'm sorry," I said. "Do you really like milk and cookies? That's kind of childish, isn't it?"

He laughed. "I'm a big kid, didn't you know that? I love milk and cookies. I love games and toys. I love having fun. That's my only acting advice for you, Charlie. Santa should always have fun."

"Why?"

"Because what I do matters."

"To whom?"

"Santa's job, Charlie, is to make children happy and show them the wonder and kindness of the world."

"Is that why you give gifts?"

"The gifts are only a part of it. A small part." He smiled. "Remember the wonder of Christmas morning, Charlie?"

I thought of standing at the top of the stairs first thing in the morning, staring down at the Christmas tree. I held my breath in anticipation.

"Remember the excitement of Christmas Eve, when you laid awake for hours, unable to sleep?"

"Of course."

"Remember the toys?"

"Well, a few . . . I remember a toy soldier. And a fishing pole from Uncle Walter . . ."

"It's not the toys that matter, is it, Charlie? It's the wonder. That's what the *Christmas Spectacular* is about: the magic children feel on Christmas morning."

I sat down at my kitchen table, which was just a little folding tray with one chair. "Is that what you're here to tell me?"

He laughed. "Charlie, I'm here to dance."

"What?"

"I've been watching the rehearsals. I love that song 'Santa's Gonna Rock 'n' Roll.' Do you think you could teach me to dance like that?"

CHAPTER
11

We think of Santa bustling through his workshop and checking on his elves; packing his sleigh and calling to his reindeer; sliding down the chimney and making sure each stocking is stuffed. But dancing? Yes, he's supposed to be a spry, jolly old elf, but he's also a portly guy. Surely that big belly wasn't made for dancing?

Well, let me tell you, Santa can dance. And not only that, most nights he was dancing long after I was pooped. A few nights, I even woke up to find him trying out some new moves in my kitchen.

"Saw this online, Charlie. What do you think?"

"Good night, Santa. Go home."

But let me back up, because this all started with a song. In the show, after Mat Mat the Insane Reindeer pulled Santa and his sleigh offstage, a cartoon video showed Santa flying through the ice and snow to the roof of Radio City Music Hall. Then, after a short pause to say good-bye to the reindeer, I ran onstage with a ho-ho-ho and told the story of my trip to New York City, "a magical place to be at Christmas." And even though "the trip coming in left some ice on my skin," I was happy now because I could warm myself with singing and dancing at Radio City Music Hall.

And since this was a musical spectacular, that story was actually a song: "Santa's Gonna Rock 'n' Roll."

And it worked. We had a full choir onstage, and it was pure magic when everyone was twisting, shouting, and singing along.

But there was one problem. And the more we rehearsed, the more that problem bothered me. "Stop, stop, stop," the director finally shouted one day. "Come here, Charles." He put his arm around me. "What's the problem, Santa? This is the best part of the show."

"I know," I said. "This is Santa's big moment. But . . . it's not his moment, if you know what I mean."

"Charles," he said, "I have no idea what you mean."

"Well, this is rock 'n' roll, right? And Santa is the lead singer. In a rock band, the lead singer is always out front, talking with the crowd, being the center of attention, doing this own thing. But I'm just . . . I mean, Santa . . . he's just dancing with the rest of the choir, doing the same moves as everyone else."

The director rubbed his chin. "Okay, Charles," he said, "let's see what you got."

I went home and practiced for a week. I started with an Elvis Presley hip swivel. Thank you, thank you very much.

Then I added a tap dancing move, like Sammy Davis Jr.

Pretty soon I was doing Chuck Berry and Michael Jackson. Santa must have been watching me dancing at home in front of my mirror.

"I like that James Brown," he said. So we watched a bunch of videos and figured out a few of James's moves.

Right there, in my apartment, Santa Claus did the splits. I told you, the guy can dance.

The more Santa and I worked on dance moves together, the more I felt the spirit of "Santa's Gonna Rock 'n' Roll." And the more the director loved it. By the end of rehearsals, I was not even sure what moves I was doing. I was just shouting and twirling, twisting and shaking, and swiveling my fake belly right to the center of the stage, in the spotlight, until I ended the song huffing for breath and pointing at the ceiling like John Travolta in *Saturday Night Fever*.

"Bravo, Charles," said the company manager, Linda Lemac. "Bravo."

Bumpy the stagehand slapped me on the back. Petey, too. David motioned me to the wings of the stage. "Don't tell anybody where you got these," he said, slipping something into my hands.

I put a finger to my nose, like I'd always seen Santa do in the movies, and slipped into the corner to see what David had given me. I couldn't believe it: candy-cane-striped sunglasses! The rock 'n' roll Santa costume was complete.

When I got home that night, I was exhausted. I felt like I'd danced a marathon. All I wanted to do was fall into a chair.

But, of course, it was already taken. Santa was there in my big comfy chair, watching football and eating spaghetti with red sauce. Half the sauce was on his shirt, which maybe was why he started wearing red in the first place. Santa wasn't too tidy.

"You did it," he said through a mouthful of noodles.

I sat down on the floor, too tired to think about the show. "Who's winning?" I asked finally, pointing at the television.

"Oh, I don't know," Santa said. "Does it matter?"

CHAPTER
12

The he problem wasn't the dancing, it was the flying. The harness was tearing at my legs every time Randy lifted me, and the more Scrooge flew, the worse the pain.

"I'm not going to make it," I told David, who had become my first friend in the show, as we left rehearsal one day. "My legs are killing me."

"I know what you mean," he said, and for the first time I noticed he was limping. "Stupid elf shoes."

"Well, the shoe must go on," I said, laughing.

The next day, I wasn't laughing when I told Abbey, the Ghost of Christmas Present, "I think Randy is out to get me. I think he's jerking the wires on purpose."

"Oh, Charles, I don't think so," she said. "Randy is a sweetheart. I don't know why he'd do that."

But I had seen the look in Randy's eyes: the way he

watched me, looking for a weakness. I'd seen the same thing with my brother. Abbey was naive if she thought there was a cause behind bullying. I knew there didn't have to be a reason.

"I can't do it," I finally told the director. We'd been working for hours, it was late, and I was miserable. "I'm sorry. I can't fly."

"Of course you can," he said. "Acrobats do it all the time."

"I'm not an acrobat."

"Abbey does it."

It must have been the pain, I tell myself now, although it was probably the Scrooge in me. It certainly wasn't any part of the Santa in me that burst out, "Who cares about Abbey? She's the Ghost of Christmas Present. She's a small part. I'm Scrooge! I have to sing. I have to dance. Everyone has to love me."

I threw down the harness and limped out the door. The streets of Manhattan had been cleaned up quite a bit since I arrived. *The Phantom of the Opera* and *Les Mis* were on Broadway, and all around me the Great White Way was shining with lights. But I didn't notice any of it. I was so embarrassed by my outburst all I noticed were the tourists. "Out of my way," I cried as I pushed through this new Times Square. "Go home, everybody. Go home. Get lost."

By the time I had made it up all five flights of stairs to my apartment, my legs were throbbing. I threw open the door, and Santa was sitting at my table in candy cane pajamas with a worried look on his face, having an animated conversation over milk and cookies with someone who looked a lot like David.

But I had just left David at the theater, so it couldn't have been him.

"Hello, Charles," Santa said. "Come and sit with me for a while."

He pushed back the second chair, which was now empty. I flopped down into it, thinking, *You're flipping out, Charlie. You're losing it. First you're seeing Santa, now you're imagining David. You're cracking up, Charlie. You're letting the pressure get to you. And the pain. This terrible pain in your legs . . .*

While I muttered, Santa just quietly stared at me, eating his favorite cookie, chocolate chip. Even though he tries to eat oatmeal raisin for his health, he always comes back to chocolate chip.

"You know, you don't have to be Scrooge," he said when he had finally finished munching. "Not forever, anyway. That's not who you are."

Before I could say anything, the doorbell rang. I looked at the door, and when I looked back, Santa was gone. There was only an empty cup of milk on my kitchen table.

"Hi," Abbey said when I opened the door. "I thought you might want to talk."

She seemed so genuinely kind that the apology just slipped out. "I'm sorry about what I said, Abbey. It wasn't nice. And it wasn't true."

"I don't care about that, Charlie," she said. "I just want to make sure you're okay. You seem stressed out."

She was right. I hadn't slept well in weeks.

I stepped aside and motioned her into the apartment. I saw her eyes scan the small room, then stop on the two cups on the table. Two cups?

"You drink milk?" she asked, clearly surprised. "I thought that was a kid's drink."

I turned, and when I looked at her, I could almost feel the twinkle in my eye. "Well, didn't you know? I'm just a big kid at heart."

CHAPTER
13

CHAPTER

13

B y the time I lay down that night, I could barely
move. *I can't do it,* I thought. *I can't keep flying.*

I thought of Santa's words: *you don't have to be
Scrooge.*

But how? I wondered. How can I be Santa if I'm not
Scrooge? Looking back, just that question was a huge
change. I had only taken the Santa part because I
wanted to be Scrooge; now it was Santa whom I really
wanted to be.

When I finally fell asleep that night, I didn't dream
about Santa—I dreamed about my Uncle Walt. He
wasn't a surrogate father to me. In fact, we didn't spend
that much time together. I remember standing in the
front yard playing army men all by myself, and Walter
would drive up and yell, "How's it going, Charlie?" as

he hurried into the house. No real father would ever leave a small boy alone like that.

But Uncle Walt was always there when I needed him. When Dad didn't show up for the father-son Boy Scouts camping trip, it was Uncle Walt who drove up in the middle of the night so I wouldn't be alone. When Mom finally kicked Dad out, it was Uncle Walt who came by every evening for two weeks to see how we were doing. When Dad died five years later in a halfway house, neglected and nearly forgotten, it was Uncle Walt who took me fishing for a few days.

And it was Uncle Walt, I remembered, who drove four hours to Murray State University the summer I graduated to talk with me about acting.

I had a degree in acting and education, and my mother cried when I told her I wasn't going to take a teaching job.

"Acting isn't a job," she said. "You can't raise a family on acting. It's just . . . Acting is just a hobby . . . for musical types."

"I'm sorry, Mom," I told her. "I've already signed the contract for summer theater."

When my uncle showed up a week later, I knew she

had sent him. And I knew she was back to crying herself to sleep because another man in the family had broken her heart.

So I was nervous when I walked over to Uncle Walter after a rehearsal for our first play. He stretched out his fist. "Take this," he said.

It was a roll of twenty-dollar bills. "It's the freedom to do what you want."

"But this is what I want," I said. He looked at me like I was out of my mind. Uncle Walter was a drill press operator, and I don't think he really understood.

"It's all I want," I said.

He reached out again and took back his money. "Then do it," he said. "And don't worry about your mama. She'll be fine. And for God's sake, don't worry about the money. This stuff ain't worth it."

I woke up. I was in my apartment in Manhattan, and sunlight was shining through the window, but I could still feel that lump of money in my hand.

A few hours later, I told John Lemac, "I'm not going to wear it," when he brought over the harness for flying practice.

John shook his head. "I don't think the director's going to like it," he said. "But you're the boss."

"I've got to do what I think is right," I told him. "And since I might be about to get fired . . . I'm not the boss. I'm sorry if I ever said I was."

I took my place onstage. I breathed deeply. Abbey came up beside me and held my hand. Across the way, Randy was sneering at me from the wings, the useless wire dangling in his hands. I just smiled.

The scene began. Abbey and I said our lines. When she started to rise, Scrooge was supposed to step onto a trunk, then onto a chair, then grab the hem of her dress and find himself lifted into the air. Instead, I stepped off the chair and, still clutching the bottom of Abbey's dress, floated across the stage on tiptoe. By the time I got to the other side, the theater was silent, waiting for the hammer to fall.

And then the voice of the director came over the loudspeaker. "Perfect," he said, "let's do it just like that."

CHAPTER
14

After that, the show came together. I can't describe it much better than to say that I felt free. I spent many of my off-hours with David and Abbey, and most of my evenings with Santa. I started having lunch with Bumpy, John, and Petey, the stagehands, and I spent a few hours one day laughing along while Eric, whom we called "The Mayor," since he had been working at Radio City for twenty years, explained how the stage went up and down in four parts, and the curtain rose and fell in twenty.

I don't remember how the Wiffle Ball games started, but by early November they were a *Radio City Christmas Spectacular* tradition during breaks in rehearsals. The auditorium was so huge it felt like a stadium, and I guess that's why someone brought a Wiffle Ball and bat. Within a week, we were running bases and keeping score. That's how big the stage is at Radio City: you can play a baseball game without worrying about anyone falling off.

And I'm pretty sure we only hit one home run into the seats the whole month.

I'd like to say we were all friends, but that's not how life works, is it? Whether it's an office, a classroom, or the North Pole, there are always a few people who don't get along with others.

Randy was still angry over the reindeer poop and a hundred other little things, I suppose. And the happier I was, and the more friends I made, the angrier he seemed to become.

He'd bump me backstage.

He'd sneer at me when no one else was looking.

One day, I could have sworn he intentionally knocked off my Santa hat right as I was about to go onstage.

"Don't worry," David told me. "It was probably an accident."

Then Randy did it again, and when I turned to say something he just stared at me. "What are you going to do?" he said.

"Don't do anything," David advised me that night. "Santa would rise above it."

I thought of my brother, and the way he always laughed when he and his friend pulled up in their truck and offered me a ride to school, then sped away when I ran up and reached for the door handle. I remembered the way, even as a kid, he laughed when he knocked me down.

I looked at David sitting on his stool. I realized for the first time how hard it probably was for him growing up in a world full of fools. I thought of the taxi cabs that drove past him, how hard it was for him to walk home at the end of every night.

"Are you okay, David?" I asked.

"These elf shoes!" He held up two green felt slippers with long curled toes and a bell on the end. "No elf would ever wear these. How could you possibly get any work done? Why, Charles?" He seemed about to say more, but then he caught himself and changed the subject. "So what are you going to do about Randy?"

"I'll do what Santa does," I smiled. "I'll put him on the naughty list."

CHAPTER
15

That night, I had a dream. It wasn't about Santa or even Scrooge. Or maybe it was about both, I'm not sure.

In the dream, I was a six-year-old child again, sitting at the old wooden table in our cramped yellow kitchen. My big brother was sitting beside me, and Mom was serving all my favorites: chicken, ham, mashed potatoes, green beans, and gravy.

"Bow your head," she said, taking her seat. "I'm going to say the blessing."

I bent my head, and even thirty years distant in my bed in Manhattan I could smell that delicious food. It was the meal we had every afternoon on Christmas Eve.

And even after all those miles and all those years, I could still feel the smack on my cheek, the one that almost knocked me into my plate. I sat up and looked at my father, who was leaning in so close I could smell the whiskey on him.

"What did you do that for?" I asked.

"You weren't listening to the prayer," he said. "You were smelling that food."

"Well, if you know that," I said, "then you weren't listening to the prayer either."

He punched me so hard I could feel all the teeth come loose in my head. I fell into my brother, who yelled, "Get off!" and pushed me back toward Dad, and the next thing I knew I was facedown on the floor.

I scrambled halfway to the kitchen door before I had the courage to stand up. I looked back, but only my father was looking at me. I ran into the living room, grabbed the Christmas globe from the little table beside Mom's chair, and smashed it to the ground. I heard the shattering of glass, but otherwise, the world was still. Nobody came to check on me. Nobody said a word.

Then I heard my father's cutlery scraping his plate as he resumed his meal.

The next thing I knew, I was outside without my hat

or coat, running up the hill in that great Kentucky snowstorm. I fell on my knees. I stared up at the sky.

I'm alone, I thought. *I'm all alone.*

I started to make a perfect snow angel. *No, I'm not alone. I'm free.*

I sat up. I looked around my small, dark apartment. I expected to see Santa Claus standing at the foot of my bed, like I'd seen him that afternoon. But nobody was there.

When I walked into Radio City Music Hall the next day, I was ready. Thirty years had passed since that Christmas Eve. Somehow I'd blocked it all out. But now I remembered. And I was going to face the bully; I was going to acknowledge my fears; and even if my father was long dead, I was going to banish his ghost once and for all. I wasn't going to let Scrooge triumph in my heart.

I walked through the backstage area, my hands clenched into fists, then around the four tiers of seating, then through three floors of dressing rooms and past the sets and wardrobes and makeup rooms and even down to the basement where Mat Mat was casually eating his prerehearsal hay.

I walked back up and stood on the stage, completely lost.

"He's gone," I heard a voice say. I looked around. They were all there: Abbey; David; John Edward, who played one of my elves; Petey; Bumpy; even John Lemac and Eric, the "Mayor of Radio City."

"What are you talking about?"

"Randy won't be bothering you anymore," Abbey said.

Somehow, I found my way to Linda Lemac's office. "What happened?" I asked.

"We let him go," she said, not even glancing up from her paperwork.

"Why?"

She looked up. "We're family, that's why."

"I'm sorry, Linda. I don't understand."

She put down her pen and looked at me for a long moment. "My goodness, Charlie," she said, "haven't you ever been in a family before?"

I don't remember much of that last dress rehearsal, but I remember giving it everything. As a child, I felt free but alone. This feeling was better. I was free and part of a family: a family of misfits, malcontents, goofballs, and musical types. What more could I want? I danced, I sang, I rode a sleigh and humbugged through London streets and trembled when the ghost told Scrooge that Tiny Tim would die. At the end, I fell on my knees and cried, "Please, spirit. Please. Give this broken man a second chance."

"That was amazing," Bumpy said as I came off the stage. "I've been here ten years and I've never seen anyone cry like that."

"I wasn't crying, Bumpy," I said. "I was acting."

He cocked his head. "What are you talking about, man? You're crying right now."

CHAPTER
16

I stayed out until two that morning, celebrating with David and Abbey and my other friends. Rehearsals were over; the show would be starting in a few days. Really, all I wanted to do till then was sleep. But when I got home, Santa was in my comfy chair, reading my copy of *A Christmas Carol*.

"Where have you been?" I said cheerfully. "I haven't seen you for a few days. I thought you were gone."

"Not unless you want me to be." He turned toward me, and I noticed he had been eating ice cream straight from the container. "You know, I didn't think this Charlie would make it either."

"Who? Charles Dickens? You knew him?"

"I take an interest."

"Anyone else I might have heard of?"

"Like Dr. Seuss? It took him four days to write the

first 90 percent of *How the Grinch Stole Christmas!*, and three months to find the right ending."

"And you were there?"

"We hung out for a while. As I did with Clement Moore, who wrote *The Night Before Christmas*."

"So that's how it works," I said, laughing. "I'm going to be rich and famous after all?"

"Well, I wouldn't say that," he said. "I have plenty of friends you've never heard of."

"It's pretty common for you to spend time away from the North Pole then?"

"Oh, once in a while, I guess, when Mrs. Claus gets annoyingly attached to someone." He paused. "I have millions of children to visit, of course, and I get to see them every year. But Mrs. Claus . . ."

"It must be hard for her, all alone at Christmas. I never thought of that."

"This year it's Stumpy," he went on. "That's what I call him, anyway. His real name is Steve. He's got Mrs. Claus convinced we shouldn't keep the naughty-and-nice list on the computer. So 'twentieth century,' he says. 'You have to keep it in the cloud.' Like I don't know what a cloud is. I see them every day!"

"So you came to help me." I felt a tingle in my fingers, just as I had when I made the perfect snow angel. "And that day, on the hill . . ."

"Oh yes, I was there."

"You kept me from being alone."

"I kept you from *feeling* alone . . ."

"But why?"

He laughed, then stuck a huge bite of chocolate chip ice cream into his mouth. "Haven't you learned anything, Charlie Hall? Don't you know who I am?"

CHAPTER
17

Opening night: the best night of an actor's life. Two months of rehearsal, and now it was here. Six thousand people would be watching, including one very special guest. I knew I probably wouldn't see him, but that didn't mean he wasn't there.

I arrived three hours early and walked the theater. Radio City had been built in the 1920s, in a grand Art Deco style. The lobby was black and gold. The silver staircases swept up to the balconies like those in a grand old house. Even the bathroom was full of magnificent, glistening tiles.

I walked into the back of the auditorium and ran my fingers along the wallpaper, with its silhouettes of musicians and singers and actors, the history of Radio City in maroon and gold. I walked up the stairs and stood in the back row of the third tier. The stagehands and set designers finishing the final details onstage looked small, but the effect of the two-hundred-foot-high vaulted ceiling made the experience enormous.

As a child, I spent time in the church. At six, I started in the choir. By twelve, I was giving sermons. It was my way of finding peace, I think, and maybe of making amends.

As I stood in Radio City that day, I felt the same way I did then: that there was something special in the building, and it lifted me. In Frankfort, Kentucky, it had been a cathedral to God. This theater, I realized, was a cathedral to art. But that didn't mean that God wasn't there as well.

I thought about all six thousand people in the audience, arranged in their careful rows. They would be here in a few hours. They would be ready for a special experience. And Santa's job was to give it to them. To become real.

I thought of the man who had visited me in Kentucky, then here in New York. I remembered his magnificent coat and his laugh that could vibrate through the heart of anyone open to it. Believe, he said, and I did. Not just in the man himself, but in all that he stood for: the wonder, the anticipation, the joy.

The show was a smash. We knew we were walking into a successful production, but I don't think any of us were prepared for the enthusiasm. The old show had been mostly Scrooge, and sure, people were fond of the old scoundrel.

But they *loved* Santa Claus.

SANTA'S BACK ON BROADWAY! the headlines shouted.

NOW THIS IS THE SPIRIT OF CHRISTMAS!

IF YOU LOVE SINGING AND DANCING, YOU'LL LOVE SANTA AND ROCKETTES! And then in smaller type: "Scrooge pretty good, too."

What can I tell you? Scrooge is a Christmas classic, but your heart wants Santa Claus, because he's magic. Even a six-thousand-person theater lights up when Santa walks in.

"Ho-ho-ho," I laughed that night. I felt the joy of Santa flowing out of me, and I felt the energy of the crowd flowing back, and I felt bigger than I'd ever felt in my life.

Other shows might teach lessons, I thought. Or

rekindle childhood memories. They might make you cry. They might make you look at the world in a more complicated way.

But that wasn't the reason for the *Radio City Christmas Spectacular*. Our show was a musical. It made you sing along. It made you dance in your seat. It lifted you up in Santa's great big arms, spun you around, and left you with the most precious gift a Broadway show can give: joy.

"Let's celebrate," Abbey and David said, bursting into my dressing room after the second standing ovation and third round of bows. "The whole cast is going."

"I've got a man to meet," I told them. "I'll catch up later."

I watched David limp off, a hand around his friend's waist for support. Then I breathed deeply and sat back in my dressing room chair. Slowly I removed my suit and beard. I heard the shouting backstage turn to talking, and then whispering, and then slowly fade away. The lights went off in the corridor.

"Good night," Linda Lemac yelled to whoever might still be around.

I waited another ten minutes, until I thought he

might not be coming. That he might not be real at all. And then he was there.

"How did I do?" I asked.

"Splendid, Charlie, splendid. Just as I knew you would."

"Any advice?"

"Advice?"

"How can I be more like Santa? What could I do better?"

"You did everything right, Charles. You sang and danced just like Santa Claus tonight, because of course you've been singing and dancing with Santa Claus for weeks."

I must have looked disappointed, because he laughed and put a hand on my shoulder. "I'm sorry if you expected more, Charlie, but you just experienced the greatest joy a person can feel: the joy of giving. There's nothing better than that!"

CHAPTER
18

But I felt there was more. I knew it. And I knew that whatever it was, it was not something Santa could teach me. I had to experience it myself. So I thought, I won't go looking. I'll just be the best Santa I can be.

And then it happened, in the middle of the fifth performance. Scrooge humbugged his way offstage, giving way to a dance number. While the Rockettes high kicked for the audience, I scurried to my dressing room to change into my Santa suit. There was a large set change, where the London city background was taken away and replaced by Santa's workshop, so after the dance the curtain went down and Santa popped out a side door yelling, "Merry Christmas! Merry Christmas, New York City!"

I pretended to brush snow from my red suit, like I'd

just come from outside. "I've traveled a long way, folks, and I need to get warm. It's time to celebrate this magical time of the year. Who wants to sing 'Jingle Bells'?"

Well, everyone of course, so I led the audience in a round of "Jingle Bells," while the conductor, Don Pippin, led the orchestra with a candy cane wand.

"Give yourselves a round of applause," I told them.

"Now I have a letter here from a little girl . . ." I started, pulling out of my pocket the letter that started the workshop scene.

A voice came over the loudspeaker. It was the stage manager. "I'm sorry, Santa. We're having a little trouble back here. Maybe you can sing 'Jingle Bells' again?"

"Well of course we can," I said, laughing merrily, and we did, bigger and louder than the first time.

And the curtain still didn't go up.

What should I do? Something was clearly wrong, and it was up to me to entertain the audience until they got it fixed. But how?

What, I wondered, would Santa do?

And that's when I saw her: a little girl in the fourth row. She was looking at me with pure joy on her face, a joy that said: I believe.

I felt a tingling in my fingertips, just as I had on the hill in Kentucky, and as I stepped to the front of the stage it was like I was stepping right out of myself. Or maybe I was just stepping into Santa's coat.

"Are there any children here tonight who want to come up and say hello to Santa Claus?"

I smiled at the girl, and motioned her forward with a friendly wave. It felt as if I was drawing her onstage with me, as if something in Santa's invitation was impossible to resist. I stepped down into the audience and took her hand. I saw another little girl and waved her forward, too. Then a boy. We sat on the edge of the stage together, in a small spotlight, while six thousand people watched from the shadows.

"What would you like for Christmas?" I asked the first girl.

She stared at me, too overwhelmed to speak.

"Don't worry," I said. "Santa knows. He always knows. And what about you?" I asked, turning to the second girl.

"A game," she said.

"To play with your little sister?" I had noticed another girl beside her in the audience, and I guessed who she was. But the little girl didn't know that, and her eyes got wide with wonder.

"And what about you?" I said, turning to the boy. "Have you been a good boy this year?"

"No," the boy snapped.

"Ho-ho-ho," I laughed. "Well now, you must be a New Yorker."

The audience laughed, and in that laughter I felt the universe open. Those may have been the best five minutes of my life, which is funny to say, because I don't even remember them. The children and I talked, but I can't recall most of what we said. A silence seemed to settle around us, the magic of the theater—no, the magic of Christmas—and those three children and I stepped out of the world and into a wonderland.

Until the stage manager said, "Okay, Santa, we're ready. It's time to go."

"Oh my, children, they're rushing Santa off," I said. "I'd love to stay, but I have work to do this time of year."

I waved then back to their seats, then read the letter, up went the curtain, and seven and a half minutes later, David rolled out of the cupboard and brought the house down.

"You did it, Charles," the director said afterward, wrapping me in a hug. "You saved the show!"

I think I shook every hand in the building before making it to my dressing room, where Santa was waiting.

"Did you see that little girl?" I asked excitedly, peeling off my beard. "Did you see the look on her face?"

He smiled. "The magic is not the hill, Charlie. It's not the snow. It's being reminded of the joy that's all around us at all times, if we open our hearts and believe."

"That's Santa Claus?" I asked.

He reached into his coat. "I think you're ready for these," he said.

CHAPTER
19

What did Santa give me that night? What was the special gift it had taken me so long to earn?

It was letters. Santa gave me six letters, all addressed to him at Radio City Music Hall. The next day, four more arrived. Then five more the day after.

"What do I do?" I asked.

"Nothing is required except to read them," he said. "But it's important to read them all. Every single one."

For three nights, I read those letter for inspiration. I loved how the children told Santa about their lives. How excited they were to see the show. "I'm in row 53, seat 12," one little boy wrote. "I know you can see me if you look."

On the fourth night, I received a letter from a nine-year-old girl. Her mother was raising her alone, she said, and working hard every day. But they kept falling further and further behind. "Sometimes I feel ashamed about the way we live," she wrote. "But then I see all my mother is going through and the sacrifice she is making for us. I've heard her crying when she thinks I'm asleep. It breaks my heart to hear her cry."

She asked for my help. Something special for Christmas.

I thought, what can I do?

I knew that kind of sorrow. I had listened to my own mother sobbing in her bedroom, night after night, when she thought no one could hear. Nobody had been able to help her. Especially not me.

"Why not call her?" Santa suggested.

"But what can I say?"

Santa put his hand on my shoulder. "Nobody said it was easy, Charlie."

I didn't answer him, because I didn't know what to say. I didn't have money to give her, and that wouldn't solve her problems anyway. Not really.

Santa must have read my mind. "You don't have to solve her problems, Charlie," he said. "I mean that sincerely. Santa Claus is not an answer. He's a friend."

The girl had provided her phone number, but I was

a coward. I didn't call, and I felt so ashamed that for a few days I stopped reading all the letters I received from children. I stopped going out to dinner with David and Abbey.

Then late one night, as I was watching television, David Letterman asked his guest Tracey Ullman what she was doing while in New York.

"I'm taking my daughter to the *Radio City Music Hall Christmas Spectacular* tomorrow night," she said. "Mabel is so excited to see Santa Claus."

I felt that old tingle, like fingertips in the snow, and sat upright in my chair. The letter, I thought. The following night, when I read the letter from the little girl to start the Santa's workshop scene, I didn't say, "Your friend, Emily."

I said, "Your friend . . . Mabel."

I received a note from Tracy Ullman the next day. "Thank you so much. You made Mabel's Christmas special. We will never forget her heart pounding through her overcoat when you mentioned her name."

I read those words again. You made Christmas special. Santa had said just one word. But that word had meant the world to a little girl.

For so long, I had been trying to make Santa bigger.

I had been picturing him as large as winter and older than snow. But at that moment, I was reminded of how small he was. Small enough to slide down a chimney. Small enough to fit in the heart of every person in the audience.

I wish I had realized that when the sad little girl wrote me her letter. I wish I had realized that Santa's power wasn't in reaching six thousand people at once; it was a word, or a smile, or a hand on the shoulder. The small gestures that reach one person and make them feel special.

It's not the billions of houses Santa visits on Christmas Eve that matter, right children? It's the fact that he cares enough to come to your house.

After Mabel, I always added a special name to the end of the letter I read on the stage. If a child wrote to say she was coming to the show, I'd say her name. If two children wrote, I'd mention them both. The next show was three. Then four. One show, I mentioned fifteen names.

That's when I realized there was a limit. One name is a memory for a lifetime. Three is still special. Fifteen was just a crowd.

"Take it slow," David told me, as we talked after the show. "There's still three weeks to go."

"Three weeks until what?"

"Until Christmas, of course."

I never called that little girl. Three weeks, and I never worked up the courage. I've kept that letter with me all these years, in a green and red box. I failed to help her, but she succeeded in helping me.

CHAPTER
20

A re you leaving?" I asked Santa one evening when I noticed an unfamiliar bag.

"I'm afraid so," he said. "It's almost Christmas, and that means there's work to be done."

"What about Stumpy?"

"Who?"

"The elf who is putting your list in the clouds."

"Oh, Steve? He's not an elf. Quite the opposite. He's a consultant."

"Well, you can't go yet," I said. "I still have a question. In fact, I have a million of them."

He stopped. "What is it, Charlie?"

I took a deep breath. "How do reindeer fly?"

Santa laughed. "Ah, so you've started meeting the children."

"They have the craziest questions," I said, plopping

down into my comfy chair. "How do they come up with them?"

"They're children, Charlie. They're more clever than we are. "

"Do you have a favorite elf?" I asked.

"Oh, Binky, I suppose. But only because he's the baby."

"The elves have babies!"

"Of course."

We sat together for hours, me asking questions and Santa answering, until I was pretty sure I'd covered everything. Until the next day, that is, when a child asked me three or four more I didn't know.

"What is your house like?" a child would ask.

"It's small and cozy," I'd say confidently, "with a gingerbread roof."

"Doesn't that get wet in the snow?"

"That's what the icing is for."

"What about the elves?"

"They don't like gingerbread. Only the bears try to eat my roof."

"But where do the elves live?"

"In the village."

"What do they eat?"

"Broccoli."

"What do you eat?"

"Cookies."

"That's not fair."

"Who said life was fair? Life is about being true to yourself."

"How long have you been Santa?"

"Longer than there have been trees."

"And what did you do before that?"

"I can't remember, because it wasn't important."

"And why do you give presents?"

"Because it makes people happy."

"How do you know what they want?"

"Sometimes I don't. Sometimes children don't even know what they want. They often change their minds when I'm already in midair. But I try to give them what they need."

"Where do you keep the reindeer?"

"I don't keep them. They're wild, but they come when I call."

"How do they fly?"

"Oh, they don't fly, my boy. They leap. They can

jump from any point on Earth to any other in the blink of an eye."

"Why isn't Rudolph here?"

"He's back at the North Pole, teaching young deer to leap. And making sure no one is mean to anyone else, no matter how different they are. We don't like bullies at the North Pole."

"You have bullies at the North Pole?"

"There are bullies everywhere, I'm afraid. But we stick together against them. We show them they are wrong, and they are only hurting themselves. Usually that works."

"Why does Frosty have to die?"

That was a new one, but it only threw old Charlie Claus for a moment.

"Don't worry, my darling," I told the girl. "Frosty doesn't die. He just goes up to heaven and waits for next year, when he returns as the fallen snow."

She smiled. Then she gave me a big hug. "I knew it," she said. "I knew it."

I reached into my bag, which I kept in my dressing room, and gave her a gift. "Merry Christmas," I said.

And what did I give all those children so they would

remember the magic once they were back out in the December cold? Candy canes? Sleigh bells?

No. I gave them my photograph. And I even signed it for them: Charles Edward Hall.

I can almost see Santa now, laughing and shaking his head, because he was watching me, you know, even when I thought he wasn't there. "Almost, Charlie Hall. You're *almost* ready."

CHAPTER
21

I wish I could tell you about all the children I met in those weeks: Zara and Gavin, Sullivan and Rachel, Isaac and Lydia, Katie and Jonah, Carrie and Sam. Also Ben, of course, and Rafi, Annabel, and Juan.

I invited so many children backstage that the security guards finally told me I had to provide a list before each show. "It's not safe," they said. "We don't know who these people are."

"I don't know who they are either," I said, laughing. "But please, let the children come. It's Christmas."

And come they did. Children of people in the show. Children of friends. Strangers I happened to meet as I walked around the theater before the show. There was the boy from the Bronx who wanted to be an actor. And the girl who came all the way from Tennessee but was too shy at first to come into my dressing room. We ended up playing "Twinkle, Twinkle Little Star" together on the piano.

"One of Santa's favorites," I told her, which I happened to know firsthand.

Then there was the naughty boy. And I don't mean ill-behaved, because that happened a lot with the children. They were so eager to meet Santa, they often forgot their manners.

No, this boy was different. He had a little sister, and I didn't like the way he yelled at her and bossed her around. I saw that not only was she hurt, but she had accepted this hurt as an ordinary part of her life. It reminded me so much of the way my brother had beaten me down and stolen my childhood wonder.

"I'm sorry, young man," I said loudly, bringing the buzz of conversation in my dressing room to a halt, "but you're a naughty boy, and you're not going to get that present you want."

He stopped and stared at me. Everybody did.

"I don't like the way you're treating your sister," I told him, "and I don't think you deserve to be on the nice list, do you?"

He didn't say anything. Neither did his grandparents,

who had brought him backstage and whose mouths were open almost as wide as his. They walked out without another word, the boy almost in tears.

For a moment, I doubted myself. I thought, *What have I done? What right do I have to tell a child what he can have for Christmas?*

"You're Santa," I heard a voice say, and I knew exactly who it was. "Of course you have that right."

"But I'm not really Santa Claus. You are."

"But it felt right, didn't it?"

I laughed. "Yes, I suppose it did."

After that, I didn't second-guess what I'd said. I had Santa's approval, and what more did I need? But it was still a relief when a few months later I received a letter from the boy's grandparents. They were writing to thank me. The boy hadn't gotten his present, and he had changed as a result. He was nicer to his sister. He was kinder to his parents. Santa hadn't given him what he wanted. Instead, the boy got what he had coming to him, and that was exactly what he'd needed.

"He's a good boy now," Santa told me many years later. "And guess what? He's also a great dad."

CHAPTER
22

Five days before Christmas, a member of our show family made a special request. Her son-in-law was an army veteran who had been injured in combat. She asked if he could come backstage and meet me.

"Does he want to meet Charles?" I asked. "Or Santa?"

"Santa," she said.

That night, the soldier came to my dressing room. His head was shaved and had a scar on the side. He was a big man, and strong, but he struggled to cross the room. His wife held his arm as you would an older person, fearing he might fall.

I felt bad for him. He looked so lost. But when he saw Santa, he smiled. And in that smile, I saw Christmas morning.

He didn't say anything. We just stood together and had our picture taken. I've gotten to know a few wounded veterans since, and I've learned that one of their strongest wishes is for the world to feel normal again. And there's nothing more comforting or comfortable than Santa Claus.

Santa is childhood. He is part of a world that was created for your happiness. And you are never, never too old to experience that joy. All you have to do is believe.

"There's some sort of magic in the suit," I told David that night. "I come to the theater every day as Charlie Hall, but by the time I put on the hat, I'm a new person. A far, far better person than I have ever been."

David nodded.

"I wish I could wear the suit every day," I told him. "How could I ever curse or shout or do anything selfish if I was wearing the suit?" He simply nodded again. "You think I'm crazy, don't you?"

"What? Who? No," he said. "It's not you. It's the boss. He's always looking over my shoulder."

"Who? The director?"

He shook his head. "Never mind," he said. He was quiet for a moment.

"Listen, Charlie," he said. "I'm proud of you. I really am. You're a heck of a Santa. Better than I thought you'd be. I guess I just thought . . . well, I thought it would be different."

"David, you never cease to surprise me."

He stepped off his stool and put on his hat, which was just a regular knit cap like everyone wears when it's zero degrees outside. "Only because you're not looking," he said with a wave. "If you're paying attention, I'm a pretty simple guy."

I started to say something, but instead I just watched him go.

"Don't mind him," Abbey said with a sly smile after David had left. "There is magic in that Santa suit. You're twice the man you were before you put it on."

CHAPTER
23

The he publicity people at Radio City were really working David and me. We made so many appearances on television talk shows and local news programs it was as if we were the unofficial New York ambassadors for the season. After a week of performances, I was dead tired, but David insisted we also make charity appearances. Children's hospitals, that was a big one for David. And orphanages. Anywhere there were children in need, David loved being there.

It was because of David that I got involved with the Garden of Dreams, an organization that granted wishes for disadvantaged and sick children. And it was through the Garden of Dreams that I met Luke. He was nine years old and he had leukemia. His wish was to meet Santa Claus. So we arranged for Luke to attend the *Radio City Christmas Spectacular.*

After the performance, he and his family came back to my dressing room. Luke walked in with a bounce in his step and a huge smile on his face. He was followed by his adorable little brother and sister, and his gracious parents. His extended family was there, too: cousins and uncles and grandparents.

"It was awesome," he said. "The show was awesome."

We talked and laughed for ten or fifteen minutes, and then of course I asked Luke what he wanted for Christmas.

"I want all these people out of the room," he said. "I want to talk with you in private."

"That sounds nice, Luke. Let's do that."

When everyone was gone, Luke came over and sat beside me. "I have a request," he said, "I want a special gift this year."

"What is it, Luke?"

"I want a Pokémon."

"Well, sure, Santa can get you a Pokémon."

"Not a toy. I want a real live Pokémon. My parents said it can't be done, but I know you can do it. You can do anything."

My heart crumpled. He was looking at me—at

Santa—so expectantly. He wanted this so badly. He believed in me, and I was going to disappoint him.

But then the words came to me. "I can't give you a Pokémon, Luke," I said, bending down and looking him in the eye. "I'm sorry. A Pokémon is a living entity, and I can't give away living things if they don't ask to be adopted first. Would it be fair for me to give your brother away if someone asked for him?"

"No," he said.

"That's because someone loves him, right? You love him. And you would miss him. It's the same with Pokémon. They have moms and dads and brothers, too. It would be wrong for me to capture one for you, even though I know you would take good care of it, Luke. Even though I want you to get your wish, because you're a good boy. Do you understand?"

"I guess so," he said.

We sat together for a while. "Is there anything else you want?" I asked.

"No," he said. "I'm okay."

He waited a minute longer, as if he was working everything out in his mind. Then he smiled. "I'm ready to go now," he said.

I put my arm around his shoulder and gave him an official photo, complete with the *right* autograph. The one he wanted: Santa C. Claus. The "C" stood for Charles. It was my way of showing which Santa I was.

"Santa is proud of you," I told him. "I've always been proud of you."

His parents were tense when they came back into the room, but when they saw the smile on Luke's face, they seemed to relax.

"Thank you, Santa," they said.

I watched the family walking away, chatting excitedly. All except Luke.

"Hold on, Luke," I yelled. He stopped. "I have something for you."

I walked over and dropped a small object into his hand. It was a sleigh bell, round and silver with a slit in one side. They were always falling off my sleigh when Mat Mat charged an elf. I had picked this one up a few days before and kept it, but until that moment I didn't know why.

"It's one of Santa's bells," I told him. "It is a reminder that my magic is always with you."

I ho-ho-hoed as they left, waving good-bye with a

smile. But when they were gone, I slumped back into my chair in my dressing room, and then I started to cry. I couldn't bear that a dying child's wish was something that no one, not even Santa, could make come true.

"I told you it wouldn't be easy," Santa's voice said when the door had closed behind them.

"I know," I said out loud, even though I was alone in my dressing room, "but you didn't say it would be this hard."

CHAPTER
24

It was an extremely cold day. So freezing, in fact, that people were waiting for the bus inside a bank lobby. The wreaths were up all over Times Square, a joyous sight, but I barely noticed as I walked to the theater in a bitter wind, still sulking from my failure with Luke. Then I noticed an older woman slip and fall on a patch of ice.

I rushed over to help her up. She was disheveled and dirty, and she had a patch over one eye. "Are you okay?"

"Yes. Thank you," she said.

"Where are you going?"

"To church."

"Then let me help you," I said, taking her arm.

"Oh no, that's all right."

"It's not a problem. I'm early for my appointment anyway."

We walked several blocks to a church and went

inside. She thanked me and walked over to talk to the priest, clearly motioning in my direction. I'm not sure why, but I decided to stay a bit. I was sitting in the back pew, watching the sunlight filter through the high empty spaces, when I noticed something in the window. It was a depiction of the saints, each in his own square of glass, and there in the bottom right corner was Saint Nicholas.

Sant-Nick-Claus.

Santa Claus.

The week before, Santa had been booked as a guest on a local television program. As I sat in the green room waiting for my scheduled time, a little girl in a red dress walked in. She was one of those young kids with adult mannerisms who chats with you in a disconcertingly mature but adorable manner. So I asked her questions about herself, and she asked me questions about myself, and finally she asked me in her very serious manner, "So how did you become Santa Claus anyway?"

I thought of Bob Yanni, the producer of the *Christmas Spectacular*, and that audition so long ago. "I was chosen," I told her.

"Yes," she said confidently. "By God."

I sat for a moment, unsure what to think. Then I laughed. At myself.

She's not talking about you, Charles Hall, I thought. She's talking about Saint Nicholas.

"Why didn't I think of this before?" I muttered to myself.

I got up from the church and hurried to Radio City Music Hall. I looked everywhere for David, but nobody had seen him. So I slipped into my dressing room and put on my Santa outfit for the opening scene with Mat Mat, Mrs. Claus, and my good friend Mr. Spruce.

"Hop on the sleigh," I whispered to David when Mr. Spruce finished clearing the crumbs from my suit.

"What?"

"When Mat Mat pulls me across the stage, hop on the sleigh and ride."

"I can't," he whispered, polishing my boots. "They want me to run alongside."

"But it hurts you."

"But I have to."

"I'll take the blame," I said.

He looked up at me.

"If they say anything, I'll take the blame. What are they going to do, fire Santa?"

David smiled as he put down his brush, and instead of running in his elf shoes, he caught a leisurely ride on the blade of the sleigh, which was an especially good thing because Mat Mat was in fine form that night, chasing poor John Edward across the stage and finally doing what he'd been dreaming of for weeks: eating his elf hat.

Nobody noticed the change.

Except David, who came out for our second scene as Santa and Mr. Spruce in a spry mood. In that one, Mr. Spruce straightened Santa's suit while I chatted with the audience. In the end, David put his hand to his chin, nodded his approval, and walked off toward the edge of the stage.

"Wait a moment, Mr. Spruce," I called.

Then I walked over, carefully straightened Mr. Spruce's jacket, and pulled the lint from his pants. "Thank you, Mr. Spruce," I said. "For everything."

David bowed to me. "Santa Claus," he said. And then he danced off the stage to spontaneous applause.

CHAPTER
25

The main question I had for Santa—the main question every child had for Santa—was how. How do you visit all the children in the world in just one night?

Santa's answer was so important that in the final weeks of rehearsal we had written it into the show. The new scene featured two brothers who couldn't find a special doll for their sister. As they were discussing what to do, they happened to pass Santa Claus ringing a bell on the street corner. He overheard their conversation and offered to take them to his workshop, where he had dozens of the dolls they were looking for. The younger brother wanted to go. The older one was skeptical.

"I just saw another Santa down the street," he challenged. "How can you be two places at once?"

"I can be in any place at any time," Santa told him.

"No you can't. You can't always be watching me, and him, and everyone," the older boy said, which was of course the second most important question children had: how did Santa make his naughty-and-nice list if he can't be everywhere?

"Oh, I'm not," my Santa replied. "Not all the time, anyway. But you never know when I'm watching. You won't recognize me, because I don't wear my suit. I'm in disguise. I may be that nice old woman you are helping, or I may be that small boy you're being naughty to."

"And how do you visit so many houses—the whole world—in one night?"

It wasn't just the leaping reindeer, I told the boys. And it wasn't just the world turning on its axis, which gave me twenty-four hours of daylight instead of twelve. "Children live second by second, one tick of the clock at a time. But there's a universe between the seconds, Thomas, where Santa and his reindeer hide. I can be anywhere in the world between one second and two. So if a wish is honest and sincere, like your wish for your sister, I am here."

The older boy wasn't convinced. But the younger boy

wanted that present. And he wanted to see the North Pole.

"Come with me then," I told him, and up we flew on invisible wires, twenty feet above the stage. It was the very thing poor old Scrooge could never do, but maybe because Randy was gone, or maybe through Santa's magic, it never hurt again.

Now the older boy believed, of course, so up he flew as well. We swooped through the air as snowflakes fell, then headed to the North Pole for a song, a dance, and that special doll. The final song, which was sung by the older boy on his return to his quiet city street, was called "Magic Is There." It was about the gift we receive when we believe, and the world of wonder that exists when you open your heart.

And my favorite detail of all: the entrance to that world was the sound of a sleigh bell.

CHAPTER
26

L uke came back. It was a few hours before the Christmas Eve show, and we were celebrating with a magnificent lasagna, bowls of spaghetti with marinara sauce, and garlic bread. It had been cooked by Bumpy's grandmother and served by the stagehands on plastic Christmas plates. We were all sitting on chairs on the stage, stuffing our faces and praising Mama Bumpy, when I noticed a colleague from Garden of Dreams signaling from the back of the auditorium.

"Can you meet with Luke again before the show?"

"Of course," I said. "I love Luke. I haven't stopped thinking about him."

An hour later I was in my dressing room in my Santa outfit when Luke walked in. I was expecting the boy I had seen a few weeks before: enthusiastic and joyous. A boy who made everyone smile. But this time, Luke looked weak. His skin had an almost bluish tint, and it seemed an effort to pull his face into a smile. He wasn't sad; he was tired. It must have been a struggle, I realized, for him to appear so healthy the first time.

"He wanted to see you again," his mother said. "He said that's all he wanted for Christmas."

"I want to talk," Luke said.

"I'd like that, Luke."

"I'm sorry for what I said last time," Luke said as soon as his mom was gone.

"But, Luke, you said nothing wrong . . ."

"I'm sorry to be so . . ." He paused. "I don't want anything this year, Santa. I wanted to tell you that. I don't want presents. I just want to be a good big brother. Because that's important. I want to set a good example for my brother and sister. They look up to me, you know."

He looked up at me. Did he know I wasn't really Santa Claus? For a moment I thought I saw disappointment, but then he smiled, and the happiness spread into his eyes. He reached into his pocket. When he opened his hand, the sleigh bell was inside. "I'm looking forward to the show," he said.

"Thank you, Luke," I said. "Your brother and sister are lucky to have you. And so am I."

He opened the door, and his mother came into the room. I hugged them both, then watched them walk down the hallway, past the other dressing rooms and the large area where the Rockette uniforms were stored on racks. As dancers and actors moved back and forth, and assistants and stage managers progressed from person to person, counting down the minutes to show time, Luke's mother put her arm around her son. Luke never glanced back. Even as the red lights blinked to signal the stage was ready, Luke and his mother stood motionless, waiting for the elevator. Then the doors opened, and they were gone.

I sat down at my dressing table and stared at the bearded man in the mirror.

"I can't do this," I said.

"You can," I heard Santa say.

I shook my head. "I'm just an actor."

"Nobody is just an actor."

I thought of that snowy Christmas Eve, the one that

plucked a heartstring for my whole life. I thought of my shadow, chasing me across the snow. "I wish Uncle Walter was here."

"I know."

"He believed in me. He was the only one."

"Not true."

"He died so young. He never even saw me as Santa Claus. But one day, when I was six . . ." I stopped and looked at myself, the man beneath the beard. "He started all of this."

"I know. I was there. I was in the window with him."

When I heard the words, I knew they were true.

"I am there whenever anyone embraces the spirit of Christmas."

I thought of what I'd been telling children when they asked how Santa knew them so well: "You never know when I'm around. You won't recognize me. I'm in disguise. But I am there."

"You're not here for me," I said. "You're here for Luke, right?"

"I'm here for both of you."

"But he is the true spirit of Christmas, not me."

"There are many ways of giving, Charlie, even if there is only one gift."

I closed my eyes. "Is he going to die?"

When I heard Santa's silence, I knew. And for a moment, I thought I would cry. Then Santa put a hand on my shoulder.

"Do you have a Christmas wish, Charlie Hall?"

"Only one."

CHAPTER
27

The performance started slowly. The first song dragged like an anchor as I tidied my sleigh and waved good-bye to my North Pole friends. As I stood offstage while the sleigh ride video played, I stared at the audience: four tiers, two hundred rows, six thousand seats.

Usually the audience inspired me. But that night, I felt the responsibility. I saw six thousands bodies leaning toward the stage, and I imagined six thousands individual faces, with a little bit of Luke in every one. How could I ever give them the happiness they came for?

Why did I ever think I could be Santa Claus?

The video ended. I stepped to the door on the side of the auditorium. I took a deep breath, opened it, and started jogging down the aisle toward the stage. I felt heavy, as if I was moving in slow motion. Where was my Christmas spirit? Where was Santa's joy?

And then I saw her: a girl in a red dress. She had squirmed free from her parents and was running toward me with her arms wide. I knelt down on one knee, stretched out my arms, and suddenly she was throwing her arms around me—"Santa Claus!"—and it felt as if the whole audience was embracing me.

We twirled around once, twice, three times, and then I set her back down. "Merry Christmas," I told her.

"Merry Christmas," I yelled to the audience, bounding to the stage. "Merry Christmas, everyone."

I'm not giving something to them, I thought as the show swirled around me, and the Rockettes kicked, and Mr. Spruce bowed. We're giving something to one another. We're creating together the special place where wonder lives.

By the time the sleigh bell rang for the little boy who believed, it really felt like I was flying. I was so deep in the magic, I could have sworn we actually had been to the North Pole.

Our script is wrong, I thought. Santa doesn't just travel the world between the seconds. He travels within all of us, all the time. When you give with love, you become Santa Claus. We all become Santa, at least for a while, when we believe in one another.

I don't remember leaving the stage that night. I remember Scrooge weeping. I remember Santa telling the world, "When you believe it, the magic is there." I remember the thunderous ovation as we came out for our curtain call. I couldn't see the individual faces in the audience, but their joy swept over me, carrying me past the other actors and actresses and into the corridors of the building and finally out the back door of the theater onto 51st Street.

It was night, and it was snowing. Big, fat flakes. I watched them whirl as I walked toward Fifth Avenue, the lights of New York City blazing around me. Ahead, I could see the bustle of Rockefeller Center Plaza, the flags flapping in the breeze, the music drifting up from the skating rink, the people crowding like penguins in the snow.

And then, suddenly, there was the famous Rockefeller Center Christmas tree, seventy feet tall and full of lights. I moved toward it, navigating through the crowd, until I was so close I had to crane my neck to see the star on top.

"I can't give you a perfect performance, you know," a voice said. "I can't win you a football game, or put you on the cheerleading squad. That's not the way it works."

"I know."

"Then why did you ask?"

"Because it was all I wanted."

I looked past the star, into the darkness, where distant constellations twinkled between the falling snowflakes.

I turned to the man beside me. Santa looked a little like Uncle Walter and a little like Mom, but also a little like Bob Yanni and Linda Lemac and David and Abbey and Petey and Luke and every other person who had meant something in my life.

Then I looked again, and he was just an old man, with a tattered jacket and a scruff of whiskers, bundled against the cold.

"It's beautiful, isn't it?" the man said.

A big snowflake fell. I held out my hand. I watched it drift into my palm, one in a million, but mine.

"Merry Christmas, son," the old man said.

"Merry Christmas, Dad," I replied.

A Fond Farewell

I t's been almost thirty years since I was chosen to play
Santa Claus for the *Radio City Christmas Spectacular*.
So much has changed. Bob Yanni, who created the
Christmas Spectacular, passed away. So did Linda Lemac,
the company manager and my good friend, after a long
struggle with breast cancer. David, my beloved Mr.
Spruce, disappeared at the end of our first season
together, never to be seen again. I heard he'd gone to
Hollywood, but I doubt that's what happened. I suspect
he's somewhere out there, explaining the true nature of
Santa Claus to someone else. My mother saw the show
only once. She died too young and broke my heart.

I still walk through Times Square every day during
the Christmas season, a place so full of drama and
spontaneity and life that it's hard to believe it's the
same Times Square from thirty years ago. I still perform

as Santa Claus four times a day for two and a half months a year, and I will until the day I can no longer walk onstage, or they finally send me home.

I live in Kentucky now during the summer. I manage a small summer stock theater with Shirley Teach Johnson, the widow of Robert E. Johnson, my old college professor and mentor, and I sit on the deck of our old lake house, as I used to sit with Mom and Uncle Walter in my childhood. Santa often visits me there and we talk long into the night. When I'm on the edge of sleep, as the stars drift on the lake, they all come to visit with me—Mom and Dad and Uncle Walter and Bob Yanni and Linda Lemac and Luke, the ones I lost—and I welcome them home.

Many years ago, the security guard at Radio City Music Hall knocked on my dressing room door. "I'm sorry to bother you, Charles," he said, "but there's an older woman here to see you. I told her you were busy, but she didn't want to leave. Her name is Martha Conway."

"Don't worry," I said. "Send her up."

"Hi Charlie," the woman in the doorway said nervously. "I doubt that you remember me."

"I remember you."

"Well, a long time ago, when you were a little boy, I did something stupid. When you said you wanted to be an actor in New York City, I laughed."

"I remember."

"I came to say I'm sorry."

It's been fifteen years since that day. Fifteen years of performances at Radio City Music Hall, and Martha Conway hasn't missed a year. She comes by bus from Frankfort, Kentucky, and she brings ten or twelve or even twenty people with her.

She comes to see the lights of Times Square and the famous windows at Macy's department store. She comes for Fifth Avenue and the Christmas tree at Rockefeller Center. She comes because the *Radio City Christmas Spectacular* captures so perfectly the joy and hope and beauty of the season.

And she comes to see the little boy from that dingy kitchen in Kentucky who believed with his whole heart that one day he could become the person he wanted to be.

She comes for Santa Claus.

A Note from the Author

Everything in this book is true. Some of it has been embellished, but it is all true nonetheless. All the scenes described as being in the *Christmas Spectacular* have been part of the show over the years. However, the show changes almost every season, so many of them are no longer performed. All the people mentioned in the book are real. Each has been an inspiration and help to me in my career as Santa, and I thank them all, especially my great friend and long-time acting partner David Steinberg, whom I miss to this day.

Acknowledgments

With deepest gratitude, I thank the millions of people who have attended the Radio City Christmas Spectacular over the years, for you have helped me discover Santa Claus.

Many thanks to all my wonderful friends and colleagues at Radio City Music Hall and Madison Square Garden Entertainment for their support and belief, especially Todd Lacy; Rich Claffey; Melissa Ormond, president of Madison Square Garden Entertainment; and especially Mr. James Dolan, for all his support and for always taking a moment to believe.

A special thanks to my agents: Matthew Bialer at Sanford J. Greenberger, Randy Chaplin at Chaplin Entertainment, and Peter McGuigan at Foundry Media. To Bret Witter and my editor, Jeremie Ruby-Strauss at Gallery Books, for sharing their knowledge and experience in creating this book. Special thanks to my dear friend Dan Schneider, who for years has been encouraging and supportive.

All my love and gratitude to brother, Tom, and my friends and family in Kentucky for understanding and never holding me back; to my mentors Robert E. Johnson and Shirley Teach Johnson for their continuous love, support, and wisdom from the early days on; and of course Martha Conway Risk, for that night in Walter's kitchen so long ago.

To my son, Blake, and daughter, Katie: your love has always kept me grounded.

To those past and present who have helped along this journey, I say thank you with all my heart, love, spirit and joy.